The wheels on the bus go 'round and 'round,
'Round and 'round, 'round and 'round:
The wheels on the bus go 'round and 'round,
All through the town.

My Memory Book

0-4

written and created for you

by

Edith A. Nicholls

Memories of me go 'round and 'round,
'Round and 'round, 'round and 'round:
Memories of me go 'round and 'round,
All through my life.

ABOUT THE MAKING OF THIS BOOK FOR YOU

Edith A. Nicholls is a social worker for Knowsley MBC Adoption and Fostering Service on Merseyside. She has been a social worker for over 25 years, working in education, generic social work and child protection. She now specialises in adoption support social work and has a special interest in the needs of children separated from their families, whether this be temporarily or permanent.

First published in 2006 by Russell House Publishing Ltd., 4 St. George's House, Uplyme Road, Lyme Regis, Dorset DT7 3LS. Tel: 01927-443948. Fax: 01927-442722. e-mail: help@russellhouse.co.uk www.russellhouse.co.uk

British Library cataloguing-in-publication data: A catalogue record of this book is available from the British Library.

ISBN 1-903855-79-9, 978-1903855-79-9   Printed by Alden Press, Oxford

Other books by the author
The New Life Work Model Practice Guide, 2005. *My Memory Book Age 8+,* 2006. *My Memory Book Age 4+,* 2005. *What Does Adopted Mean? A Young Child's Guide to Adoption,* 2005.

Available from Russell House Publishing, Lyme Regis, Dorset DT7 3LS. Tel: 01297 443948. help@russellhouse.co.uk

What's In This Book and Where to Find it?

Lucy Locket lost her pocket,
Kitty Fisher found it,
But ne'er a penny was there in it,
Except the binding 'round it.

Memories are precious,
Keep them safe and true.
And then when you get older
You'll see how they made you.

This is your memory book and it is about memories of you

From.............................. To..

This book was created by...(carer)
(other details)...
With help from   ....(social worker)
(other details)..
And...(birth family)
(other details)..
And ....(others)
(other details)..

I'm a dingly, dangly Scarecrow.
With a floppy, floppy hat.
I can shake my hands like this.
I can shake my feet like that.

Section 1

About Me

Who do people say I look like?

I have ten little fingers and
ten little toes,
Two little arms and one little
nose,
One little mouth and two little
ears,
Two little eyes for smiles and
tears,
One little head and two little
feet,
One little chin makes me all
complete!

What does my name mean?

Who chose my names?

Why was I given my names?

Star light, star bright,
First star I see tonight,
I wish I may, I wish I might,
Have the wish I wish tonight.

Where does my family originate from?

Who was there when I was born?

2

Other things about my birth...

Full Name

Date of Birth

Place of Birth

Day of Birth

Time of Birth

Birth Weight

Birth Length

"Twinkle, twinkle little star
How I wonder what you are.
Up above the world so high
Like a diamond in the sky."

When I was born

3

On the Day I was Born...

The most popular music was ....

The most popular TV programmes were ....

The Prime Minister and Government were ....

The most popular films were ....

The most popular books were ....

The most popular children's games were ....

Everyone was talking about ....

The top fashion was ....

In the news was ....

4

Bye, Baby Bunting,
Daddy's gone a hunting,
To get a little rabbit skin
To wrap his Baby Bunting in!

My Family

My Mum .... Date of Birth ....

Address ....

My Dad .... Date of Birth ....

Address ....

My Grandparents ....

Address ....

My Grandparents ....

Address

My brothers and sisters and where they live...

My Family Tree

MY HANDPRINTS

Don't forget to put the dates!

My ...

Personality...

Looks...

Sleeping...

Feeding...

Crawling and walking...

Crying...

Laughs and laughing...

Waking...

My toys and books...

My fears and scary things...

My music and rhymes...

My favourite things…

My absolutely un-favourite things…

Chick, chick, chick, chick, chicken,
Lay a little egg for me.
Chick, chick, chick, chick, chicken,
I want one for my tea.
I haven't had an egg since Easter,
And now it's half past three.
So, chick, chick, chick, chicken,
Lay a little egg for me.

10

And even more...

My daily routine...

My favourite kind of play...

Girls and boys come out to play,
The moon doth shine as bright as day;
Come with a whoop and come with a call,
And come with a good will or not at all.

My talents...

11

What People Said About Me...

Who said it	What they said and why

People and things	What I called them

What's your name?

"Pudden Tame."

What' your other?

"Bread and Butter."

Where do you live?

"In a sieve."

What's your number?

"Cucumber."

13

I have...	Which means...	I take this medication...

My Health and Me

Date	Hospital/Doctor/Clinic	What for and what happened?

I'm glad the sky is painted blue,
And the earth is painted green,
With such a lot of nice fresh air
All sandwiched in between!

Section 2

Being Looked After

My Day by Day Week...

On Mondays we...

On Tuesdays we...

On Wednesdays we...

On Thursdays we...

On Fridays we...

On Saturdays we...

On Sundays we...

Seeing My Family

Who I see	When I see them	Where I see them

About Seeing My Family

Stories about seeing my family

My Looked After Diary

Date	Happening	Outcome

My nursery is called ....

The address is ....

I go to my nursery on ....

I like my nursery because:- ....

These are the people who work at my nursery:-

....

....

This is what they say about me:-

Date	Name

My Playgroup

My playgroup is called ....

The address is ....

I go to my playgroup on ....

These are the people who work in my playgroup:-

My friends at playgroup are ....

I like playgroup because ....

This is what they say about me at my playgroup:-

Date	Name	

My pre-school nursery is called ....

The address is ....

I go to pre-school nursery on ....

My nursery teacher is .... My best friend is ....

My other friends are ....

This is what I like best about pre-school nursery ....

What they say about me at my pre-school nursery:-

Date	Name	

My Pre-school Nursery

When I was 2 weeks old...

I could

I weighed   My eyes were

My hair was

At bedtimes and sleepy times I would

At bath time I would

My favourite things were

My un-favourite things were

All about me at 2 weeks old

I measured

When I was 4 weeks old...

I could

I weighed   My eyes were

My hair was

At bedtimes and sleepy times I would

At bath time I would

My favourite things were

My un-favourite things were

All about me at 4 weeks old

I measured

33

When I was 6 weeks old...

I could

I weighed .... My eyes were ....

My hair was ....

At bedtimes and sleepy times I would

At bath time I would

My favourite things were

My un-favourite things were

All about me at 6 weeks old

I measured

34

When I was 8 weeks old...

I could

I weighed .... My eyes were ....

My hair was ....

At bedtimes and sleepy times I would

At bath time I would

My favourite things were

My un-favourite things were

All about me at 8 weeks old

I measured

When I was 10 weeks old...

I could ....

I weighed .... My eyes were ....

My hair was ....

At bedtimes and sleepy times I would

At bath time I would

My favourite things were

My un-favourite things were

All about me at 10 weeks old

I measured

When I was 12 weeks old...

I could ....

I weighed .... My eyes were ....

My hair was ....

At bedtimes and sleepy times I would

At bath time I would

My favourite things were

My un-favourite things were

All about me at 12 weeks old

I measured

When I was 4 months old...

I could ....

I weighed .... My eyes were ....

My hair was ....

At bedtimes and sleepy times I would ....

At bath time I would ....

My favourite things were ....

My un-favourite things were ....

All about me at 4 months old ....

I measured ....

When I was 5 months old...

I could ....

I weighed .... My eyes were ....

My hair was ....

At bedtimes and sleepy times I would ....

At bath time I would ....

My favourite things were ....

My un-favourite things were ....

All about me at 5 months old ....

I measured ....

When I was 6 months old...

I could

I weighed .... My eyes were

My hair was

At bedtimes and sleepy times I would

At bath time I would

My favourite things were

My un-favourite things were

All about me at 6 months old

I measured

When I was 7 months old...

I could

I weighed .... My eyes were

My hair was

At bedtimes and sleepy times I would

At bath time I would

My favourite things were

My un-favourite things were

All about me at 7 months old

I measured

37

When I was 8 months old...

I could

I weighed .... My eyes were ....

My hair was ....

At bedtimes and sleepy times I would

At bath time I would

My favourite things were

My un-favourite things were

All about me at 8 months old

I measured

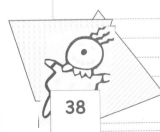

When I was 9 months old...

I could

I weighed .... My eyes were ....

My hair was ....

At bedtimes and sleepy times I would

At bath time I would

My favourite things were

My un-favourite things were

All about me at 9 months old

I measured

When I was 10 months old...

I could

I weighed .... My eyes were ....

My hair was ....

At bedtimes and sleepy times I would

At bath time I would

My favourite things were

My un-favourite things were

All about me at 10 months old

I measured

When I was 12 months old...

I could

I weighed .... My eyes were ....

My hair was ....

At bedtimes and sleepy times I would

At bath time I would

My favourite things were

My un-favourite things were

All about me at 12 months old

I measured

When I was 14 months old...

I could ....

I weighed .... My eyes were ....

My hair was ....

At bedtimes and sleepy times I would ....
....

At bath time I would ....
....

My favourite things were ....
....

My un-favourite things were ....
....

All about me at 14 months old ....
....
....

I measured ....

When I was 16 months old...

I could ....

I weighed .... My eyes were ....

My hair was ....

At bedtimes and sleepy times I would ....
....

At bath time I would ....
....

My favourite things were ....
....

My un-favourite things were ....
....

All about me at 16 months old ....
....
....

I measured ....

When I was 18 months old...

I could

I weighed   My eyes were

My hair was

At bedtimes and sleepy times I would

At bath time I would

My favourite things were

My un-favourite things were

All about me at 18 months old

I measured

When I was 2 years old...

I could

I weighed   My eyes were

My hair was

At bedtimes and sleepy times I would

At bath time I would

My favourite things were

My un-favourite things were

All about me at 2 years old

I measured

When I was 2½ years old...

I could

I weighed .... My eyes were ....

My hair was ....

At bedtimes and sleepy times I would

At bath time I would

My favourite things were

My un-favourite things were

All about me at 2½ years old

I measured

When I was 3 years old...

I could

I weighed .... My eyes were ....

My hair was ....

At bedtimes and sleepy times I would

At bath time I would

My favourite things were

My un-favourite things were

All about me at 3 years old

I measured

When I was 3½ years old...

I could

I weighed .... My eyes were ....

My hair was ....

At bedtimes and sleepy times I would

At bath time I would

My favourite things were

My un-favourite things were

All about me at 3½ years old

I measured

When I was 4 years old...

I could

I weighed .... My eyes were ....

My hair was ....

At bedtimes and sleepy times I would

At bath time I would

My favourite things were

My un-favourite things were

All about me at 4 years old

I measured

43

Memories of My 'Growing'...

In the Year I was 1 year old...

The most popular music was...

The most popular TV programmes were...

The Prime Minister and Government were...
The most popular films were...
The most popular books were...
The most popular children's games were...

Everyone was talking about...

The top fashion was...
In the news was...

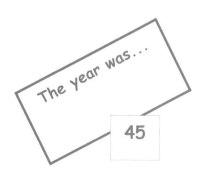

The year was...

In the Year I was 2 years old...

The most popular music was..

The most popular TV programmes were...

The Prime Minister and Government were...
The most popular films were...
The most popular books were...
The most popular children's games were...

Everyone was talking about...

The top fashion was...
In the news was...

The year was...

In the Year I was 3 years old...

The most popular music was...

The most popular TV programmes were...

The Prime Minister and Government were...
The most popular films were...
The most popular books were...
The most popular children's games were...

Everyone was talking about...

The top fashion was...
In the news was...

The year was...

In the Year I was 4 years old...

The most popular music was...

The most popular TV programmes were...

The Prime Minister and Government were...
The most popular films were...
The most popular books were...
The most popular children's games were...

Everyone was talking about...

The top fashion was...
In the news was...

The year was...

My first words were...

Date ....

I was bottle fed with...

Date ....

Mary, Mary, quite contrary, How does your garden grow?

"With silver bells and cockle shells, And pretty maids all in a row."

My first solid food was...

Did I have a dummy?

Tell me more...

My favourite T.V pro-gramme was...

Date ....

My favourite story was...

Date ....

Did I have a teddy?

Tell me more...

What did I call you?

Tell me more...

My favourite food was...

Date ....

Did I blow raspberries?

Tell me more...

My first shoes were...

Date ....

My favourite toy was...

Date ....

49

Jack be nimble
Jack be quick
Jack jump over the candlestick

Did I have naughty moments?

Tell me more...

Where did I sleep?

Tell me more...

What was I like in the mornings?

Tell me more...

Who didn't I like?

Tell me more...

50

Hickory, dickory, dock,
The mouse ran up the clock,
The clock struck one
The mouse was gone,
Hickory dickory dock.

What made me cry?

Tell me more...

Did I get sweets and treats?

Tell me more...

How did you know when I was tired?

Tell me more...

Did I have tantrums?

Tell me more...

What kind of birthday cakes did I have?

Tell me more...

51

Baa, baa, black sheep
Have you any wool?
Yes sir, yes sir three bags full.
One for the master and one for the dame
And one for the little boy who lives down the lane.

Section 4

My Firsts
and
Big Events

My 'Firsts'

I First...	Date	What happened....
Smiled		
Laughed		
Lifted my head		
Rolled over		
Crawled		
Stood up		
Walked		
Cut a tooth		
Ate solids		
Had a haircut		
Used the potty		
Said a word		
Wore shoes		
Went without my nappy		
Drank from a cup		

Other Memories of My 'Firsts'

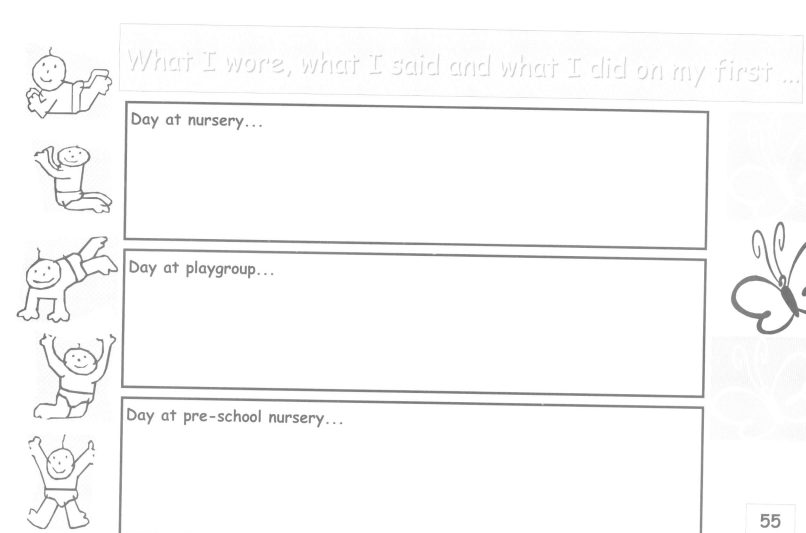

What I wore, what I said and what I did on my first ...

Day at nursery...

Day at playgroup...

Day at pre-school nursery...

When, why and how

What I would do

Date	Event or happening

If your happy and you know it clap your hands,
If your happy and you know it clap your hands,
If your happy and you know it
And you really want to show it
If your happy and you know it clap your hands.

Section 5

My Happy Birthdays,
Holidays and
Special Days of Celebration

On my 1st Birthday we ....

I got these presents ....

On my 2nd Birthday we ....

I got these presents ....

On my 3rd Birthday we ....

I got these presents ....

On my 4th Birthday we ....

I got these presents ....

Happy Birthday to you

Memories of My Happy Birthdays

These are some special memories of my Birthdays...

And more memories...

DATE:_____

Where we went ....

Who went with us ....

How we got there ....

Where we stayed ....

What we did ....

A story about me on holiday ....

....

DATE:_____

Where we went ....

Who went with us ....

How we got there ....

Where we stayed ....

What we did ....

A story about me on holiday ....

....

Other Memories of My Holidays

My Special Days of Celebration

My ethnicity is

My culture is

My religion is

These are the religious festivals my family and I celebrate...

Celebrating Special Days

Festival	How we celebrated and what it meant for me

Celebrating Special Days

Festival	How we celebrated and what it meant for me

Come to the window my baby with me,
And look at the stars that shine on the sea.
There are two little stars that play bo-peep
With two little fish far down in the deep.

Section 6

Other Memories of Me

Other Memories of Me

Date	Memory

Other Memories of Me

Date	Memory

Other Memories of Me

Date	Memory